Learning How to Appreciate Differences

Susan Kent

The Rosen Publishing Group's
PowerKids Press™
New York

For Roman and Diane Sadowy, in appreciation of everything.

Published in 2001 by The Rosen Publishing Group, Inc.
29 East 21st Street, New York, NY 10010

First Edition

Book Design: Maria E. Melendez

Photo Credits: Cover and title page, pp. 4, 7, 8, 11, 12, 15, 16, 19, 20 by Myles Pinkney.

Kent, Susan, 1942–
     Learning how to appreciate differences / Susan Kent.— 1st ed.
        p. cm.— (The violence prevention library)
     Summary: Discusses how to appreciate differences in people, emphasizing the importance of following your interests, deciding what you like, standing up for yourself, and appreciating others.
     ISBN 0-8239-5617-2 (acid-free paper)
     1. Toleration—Juvenile literature. 2. Difference (Psychology)—Juvenile literature. [1. Toleration. 2. Prejudices.] I. Title. II. Series.

HM 1271 .K46 2000
179.9—dc21   00-027184

Manufactured in the United States of America

Contents

We Are All Different

No two people are exactly alike. We are all different. You probably have some things in common with others, though. You may be tall like your uncle Peter or a fast runner like your mom. You and your best friend might like the same kind of music. No one is exactly like you, though. You are one of a kind! You may enjoy the things you have in common with other people. It can be comfortable to be part of a group. It is also important to **appreciate** the things that make you different. It is **variety** that makes the world interesting.

You may have things in common with others, but no two people are exactly alike.

Hank

Hank is a good student and a good **athlete**. He is the best fielder and base runner on his team. He likes the excitement of a good baseball game. Hank also likes to dance. Watching dancers on television makes him happy. He asks his parents for dance lessons. Although his cousins laugh at him, Hank loves taking dance lessons. He practices hard and becomes a good dancer. When his cousins see him dance in a **recital**, they are proud of him.

Hank is glad he is following his dreams. ▶

Following Your Interests

Some people know exactly what interests them. You may love studying butterflies. Maybe basketball is your passion. You may enjoy collecting stamps or drawing. If you know what you like to do most, go for it! Many people, though, do not have just one thing they enjoy doing. Perhaps you like to ride your bike and go fishing in the creek. Maybe you like playing with your dog and spending time with your family. All of these activities are fun. It is important to do activities that interest you.

◀ *You should spend time doing activities that you enjoy.*

Deciding What You Like

Only you know what you like and do not like to do. However, other people can give you ideas. Your parents may suggest you take piano lessons. Friends might urge you to join a hockey team. Your teacher may invite you to join the chess club. When you see a friend doing gymnastics, you might think it looks like fun. Pick something that interests you, and give it a try. See how you like it. You do not have to decide right away, though. New things often seem hard at first, but you might end up liking them. Only you can decide what is right for you.

Joining clubs and trying new things are good ways to find activities that interest you. ▶

Being Different

Not everyone enjoys the same activities or the same subjects. You may love math and dislike reading. Your best friend may be just the opposite. He may like reading but not math. You may think science experiments are great. Your friends may not like science class. They may be counting the minutes until gym class. Never be **embarrassed** about what you like. Do not feel afraid to do what interests you even if other people are not interested. Be proud of your own interests and your own special abilities. Be proud of who you are.

Everyone has different interests. You should never feel embarrassed about what you like to do.

Sally and Sharon

Sally and Sharon have a lot in common. They are both crazy about animals. They love to visit pet stores and the zoo. They also love to ride their bikes and climb trees. They talk on the phone for hours and share secrets. Sally and Sharon also have different interests. Sally plays the violin. She spends hours practicing. Sharon plays soccer. She is the goalie for her team. Sally comes to all Sharon's games and cheers for her. When Sally performs, Sharon is there leading the clapping. Sally and Sharon are best friends.

Sally and Sharon have a lot in common, but they also enjoy separate activities. ▶

Standing Up for Yourself

Everyone wants to be liked. You may worry that your classmates won't like you if you are different. You may be afraid they will laugh at you. You may feel **pressure** from friends to do what they like. Though you may want to try activities your friends suggest, never give up doing what interests you. Don't try to be someone else! When you stand up for yourself and follow your own dreams, you feel good about yourself. Your friends will like you for being who you are. Your classmates will **respect** you for your own special abilities.

◀ *This boy enjoys spending time playing the piano.*

Appreciating Others

You are not the only one who is different, you know! You are **unique**, but so is everyone else. Be sure to appreciate the differences in other people. If you like sports, try to get to know someone who likes music. If painting is your thing, spend some time with kids who love science. You can learn about each other's interests. Introduce yourself to new kids in your school. Perhaps they just came here from another country. You might find it interesting to learn about their **customs**. You may discover you have a lot in common.

You might be surprised by the things you can learn from other people. ▶

Standing Up for Others

Sometimes kids who are different get picked on or teased. They may be kept out of activities. If something like this has happened to you, you know how bad it feels. Try to make sure it never happens to anyone in your school. If you see classmates sitting alone during recess, invite them to join your game. When you see kids being picked on, whether by one person or a group, stand up for them. Try to get the bullies to stop. If you can't do it on your own, get together with your friends to **defend** anyone who is being hurt.

◀ *This girl is helping her classmate pick up books from the floor.*

Marsha and Reynaldo

Reynaldo is sitting alone in the lunchroom when some boys come over and laugh at the food his mother packed for him. They knock his lunch off the table. Marsha helps Reynaldo pick it up. She then invites him to sit with her. Marsha and Reynaldo discover that they both play soccer and that they live near each other. They decide to walk to school together. On their walks to school, Marsha helps Reynaldo with his English. He starts teaching her Spanish. Marsha and Reynaldo become good friends.

Glossary

appreciate (uh-PREE-shee-ayt) To be thankful for something or someone.

athlete (ATH-leet) A person who is skilled in sports.

customs (KUS-tumz) The accepted, respected ways of doing things that are passed down from parent to child.

defend (dih-FEND) To protect from attack or harm.

embarrassed (im-BAYR-ist) Feeling uncomfortable or ashamed.

pressure (PREH-shur) A strong influence or force.

recital (ree-SY-til) A show given by musicians or dancers.

respect (ree-SPEKT) To think highly of someone or something.

unique (yoo-NEEK) One of a kind.

variety (vuh-RY-ih-tee) Many different kinds of things.

Index